TOP 10 SAR

TRAVEL GUIDE

The Complete Guide to Memorable Journeys, Undiscovered Wonders, and Timeless Beauty

Nigel Winter

INTRODUCTION TO SARDINIA

Welcome To Sardinia

As soon as I stepped foot on the sandy shores of Cagliari, the capital of Sardinia, my voyage had officially begun. A soft breeze bringing the aroma of the sea and the lyrical sounds of the Italian language met me as soon as I exited the airport. It seemed as though the island itself was promising a unique experience while narrating tales of its colorful past.

I experienced a time travel while exploring Castello,

Cagliari's historic district, on its winding cobblestone lanes. The atmosphere was permeated with a tangible feeling of history thanks to the medieval architecture, quaint cafés, and bustling markets. I stumbled upon the grand Cagliari Cathedral, standing proudly as a tribute to the island's religious heritage, as I was meandering through the city's labyrinthine passageways.

I left Cagliari and headed north to the untamed beach that Sardinia is renowned for. The Costa Smeralda's green waves called to me, offering peace and unspoiled beauty. My breath was taken away at the sight of the glistening sea set against the majestic granite cliffs. I was compelled to jump into the glistening waves and submerge myself in the wild surroundings.

The many landscapes of Sardinia spread before me like a wonderful tapestry as I continued traveling. Each part of the island had its own distinct appeal, from the gently undulating hills of the interior, dotted with vineyards and olive groves, to the windswept beaches of the west coast. I was mesmerized by the strange rock formations of Capo Testa and the captivating location of Su Nuraxi, where I became engrossed in the earliest mysteries of the Nuragic culture.

Sardinia impressed me with its unadulterated beauty and classic attractiveness. My soul had been permanently changed by the rich tapestry of natural wonders, history, and culture that it contains. I knew as I said goodbye to this island paradise that Sardinia would always hold a particular place in my heart and be a destination I anxiously looked forward to visiting again to make new memories and discover more of its mysteries.

History and Culture

At the heart of Sardinia's history lies the enigmatic Nuragic civilization, which thrived on the island from the Bronze Age to the Roman conquest. The Nuragic people left behind an astonishing legacy of stone towers called nuraghi, which stand as silent witnesses to their sophisticated architectural prowess. These megalithic structures, some reaching heights of over 20 meters, offer a glimpse into a civilization shrouded in mystery, evoking awe and curiosity among historians and visitors alike.

In the centuries that followed, Sardinia became a coveted prize for various Mediterranean powers, each leaving their mark on the island's cultural fabric. The Phoenicians, Carthaginians, Romans, Byzantines, and Spanish, among others, all contributed to the island's cultural mosaic. This diverse heritage can be seen in the architecture, language, and traditions that have endured through the ages.

One of the most striking aspects of Sardinian culture is its language, Sardo, which is distinct from Italian and showcases the island's ancient roots. Traditional festivals and celebrations, such as the lively carnival of Mamoiada and the solemn Holy Week processions in Cagliari, offer glimpses into the island's deep-seated traditions and religious fervor.

Music and dance also play a significant role in Sardinian culture. The haunting melodies of the launeddas, a traditional woodwind instrument, echo through the air, transporting listeners to a bygone era. The intricate footwork of traditional dances like the su ballu tundu captivates audiences, preserving the island's cultural heritage in rhythmic motion.

As I delved into Sardinia's history and culture, I marveled at the island's ability to retain its distinct identity amidst changing

tides. It is a testament to the resilience and pride of the Sardinian people, who have safeguarded their traditions and embraced their past while embracing the present.

Sardinia's history and culture are like the threads of a tapestry, intricately woven together to create a mesmerizing tableau. Exploring the island's ancient ruins, engaging in local festivities, and immersing oneself in its vibrant traditions is a transformative experience, allowing visitors to connect with a timeless heritage that has shaped Sardinia into the captivating destination it is today.

Geography and Climate

The geography of Sardinia is characterized by a rugged coastline that stretches for over 1,800 kilometers (1,118 miles), adorned with stunning beaches, secluded coves, and dramatic cliffs. Along the northern coast, the renowned Costa Smeralda captivates with its emerald waters and pristine sandy shores, while the western coast showcases untamed beauty with towering cliffs, hidden caves, and windswept dunes. In the south, the landscape transforms into a tapestry of lagoons, salt marshes, and flamingo-filled wetlands, offering a haven for birdwatching and wildlife enthusiasts.

As one ventures inland, Sardinia unveils a different facet of its geography. The island is dominated by a series of mountain ranges, including the Gennargentu Massif in the east, which is home to Sardinia's highest peak, Punta La Marmora. The mountainous interior is a haven for hikers and nature lovers, offering breathtaking vistas, deep valleys, and ancient forests that are home to unique flora and fauna.

The climate of Sardinia is Mediterranean, characterized by hot, dry summers and mild, wet winters. Summers are long and sunny, with temperatures often exceeding 30°C (86°F), making it an ideal destination for beachgoers. Spring and autumn bring milder temperatures, while winters are generally mild but can be wet, especially in the northern and mountainous regions.

Sardinia's diverse geography and climate contribute to a rich and varied ecosystem. The island is known for its endemic plant species, such as the Sardinian daffodil and the Sardinian peony, as well as its unique wildlife, including the Sardinian deer and the mouflon, a type of wild sheep. The marine environment surrounding the island is also teeming with life, offering opportunities for snorkeling, scuba diving, and exploring vibrant underwater ecosystems.

GETTING TO SARDINIA

Best Time to Visit

One of the most popular times to visit Sardinia is during the summer months, from June to September. During this period, the island basks in warm sunshine, and the azure waters beckon visitors for refreshing dips. The beaches come alive with activity, and beach clubs and seaside resorts buzz with energy. July and August are particularly busy months, attracting both international travelers and locals seeking a summer getaway. It's important to note that during peak season, popular tourist destinations may be crowded, and prices for accommodations and activities tend to be higher. However, the vibrant atmosphere, long days, and lively beach scenes make it an ideal time for sun worshippers and water sports enthusiasts.

For those seeking a more tranquil and budget-friendly experience, the shoulder seasons of spring and autumn offer favorable conditions. From April to June and September to October, the weather is pleasant, with mild temperatures and fewer crowds. Nature enthusiasts will appreciate the blooming wildflowers in spring, while autumn brings a palette of vibrant colors to the island's landscapes. It's an excellent time for hiking, exploring archaeological sites, and immersing oneself in the island's cultural heritage. During these months, accommodations and flights are often more affordable, and popular attractions are less crowded.

Winter, from November to February, is the quietest period on the island. While the temperatures are cooler, ranging from 10°C to 15°C (50°F to 59°F), Sardinia still has a charm of its own during this time. The island's natural beauty takes on a different allure, and visitors can enjoy peaceful walks along the beaches, visit local markets, and indulge in traditional Sardinian cuisine. Winter also offers the opportunity to experience local festivals and cultural events.

Ultimately, the best time to visit Sardinia depends on your personal preferences and the experiences you seek. Whether you long for a lively beach holiday, a serene nature retreat, or a cultural immersion, Sardinia's diverse seasons ensure that there is something for everyone, all year round.

Getting to Sardinia

By Air

Cagliari-Elmas Airport, located near the capital city of Cagliari in the south, serves as the main international gateway to Sardinia. It offers numerous direct flights to major European cities, including Rome, Milan, London, Frankfurt, and Barcelona, among others. Many reputable airlines operate regular flights to Cagliari, providing travelers with a wide range of options when planning their journey. The airport is well-equipped with modern facilities and amenities, ensuring a smooth arrival and departure experience.

Another major airport in Sardinia is Olbia Costa Smeralda Airport, situated in the northeast region of the island. Olbia is a popular entry point for visitors heading to the renowned Costa Smeralda and other scenic destinations in the region. The airport offers both domestic and international flights, connecting Sardinia with various European cities, including Rome, Milan, Zurich, Paris, and Amsterdam, to name a few. With its strategic location, Olbia provides convenient access to the stunning beaches and resorts of the Costa Smeralda.

Alghero-Fertilia Airport, located in the northwest, is another option for travelers looking to reach Sardinia by air. It offers domestic and international flights, primarily connecting with Italian cities such as Rome, Milan, and Venice, as well as destinations in Europe, including Barcelona, London, and Brussels. Alghero Airport serves as a gateway to the scenic northwestern coast, renowned for its rugged beauty, historic towns, and ancient ruins.

Upon arrival at any of the airports in Sardinia, travelers can easily access their desired destinations using various transportation options. Car rental services are available at the airports, allowing visitors the freedom to explore the island at their own pace. Additionally, taxis, shuttle buses, and public transportation are readily accessible, providing convenient connections to major cities, towns, and resorts.

Getting to Sardinia By Ferry

Ferry services to Sardinia operate from various ports along the Italian mainland, such as Genoa, Livorno, Civitavecchia, and Naples, as well as from neighboring countries like France and Spain. The availability and frequency of ferry routes may vary depending on the season, so it's advisable to check schedules and book in advance, especially during peak travel periods.

The journey to Sardinia by ferry offers a captivating experience, allowing you to soak in the stunning coastal scenery and enjoy the tranquility of the sea. As the ferry glides through the azure waters, you can relax on deck, savoring the gentle breeze and panoramic views. Some ferries even provide onboard amenities, including restaurants, cafes, shops, and comfortable seating areas, ensuring a pleasant and convenient voyage.

The duration of the ferry journey to Sardinia depends on the departure port and the type of ferry you choose. Routes from the Italian mainland typically range from 6 to 12 hours, while longer routes from destinations like France or Spain may take around 10 to 20 hours. Overnight ferry options are also available, allowing you to sleep onboard and wake up to the beauty of Sardinia's shores.

Arriving by ferry offers the advantage of bringing your own vehicle, which is particularly convenient for exploring the island independently. Sardinia has an extensive road network, and having a car allows you to venture off the beaten path and discover hidden gems at your own pace.

Upon reaching Sardinia, the ferries dock at various ports, including Cagliari, Olbia, Porto Torres, and Arbatax, offering easy access to different parts of the island. From there, you can embark on your Sardinian adventure, whether it's discovering historic sites, basking on pristine beaches, or immersing yourself in the island's vibrant culture.

ACCOMMODATION IN SARDINIA

Hotels and Resorts

- **Hotel Capo d'Orso Thalasso & SPA** is a 5-star hotel located in the north of Sardinia. It has stunning views of the sea, and it's surrounded by lush vegetation. The hotel has a private beach, a spa, and several restaurants. €500 per night
- **Hotel Cala di Volpe**, a Luxury Collection Hotel, Costa Smeralda is another 5-star hotel located in Sardinia. It's situated on a private cove, and it has its own beach. The hotel has two restaurants, a bar, and a spa. €700 per night

- **Resort Valle dell'Erica Thalasso & SPA** is a 4-star hotel located in the northeast of Sardinia. It's surrounded by pine trees and has a private beach. The hotel has a spa, several restaurants, and a golf course. €400 per night

Villas and Vacation Rentals

Villa L'Arco

- Location: Luogosanto, Province of Sassari

Nightly rate: €3,500

- Highlights: This stunning villa is located in a secluded spot in the mountains of Sardinia, with stunning views of the surrounding countryside. It has six bedrooms, six bathrooms, a large swimming pool, and a private garden.

Villa I Pini

- Location: Pula, Metropolitan City of Cagliari
- Nightly rate: €2,500
- Highlights: This luxurious villa is located in the heart of the Costa Smeralda, with easy access to some of the island's most popular beaches. It has five bedrooms, five bathrooms, a large swimming pool, and a private garden.

EXPLORING CAGLIARI

Cagliari Old Town

One of the most popular things to do in Castello is to explore the narrow streets and alleyways. These streets are lined with shops, cafes, and restaurants, and there are always people milling about. It's a great place to wander aimlessly and get lost in the atmosphere.

Another popular activity in Castello is to visit the many historical buildings. These include the Cathedral of Santa Maria, the Palazzo Regio, and the Bastione di Saint Remy. The cathedral is a beautiful example of Pisan-Romanesque architecture, while the

Palazzo Regio was once the home of the royal family of Savoy. The Bastione di Saint Remy is a defensive wall that offers stunning views of the city and the surrounding countryside.

In addition to its historical attractions, Castello is also home to a number of museums. These include the National Archaeological Museum, the Museum of Cinema, and the Museum of the Mediterranean. The National Archaeological Museum houses a collection of artifacts from Sardinia's ancient past, while the Museum of Cinema is dedicated to the history of film in Sardinia. The Museum of the Mediterranean is a more recent addition to the city's cultural scene, and it explores the cultural and environmental heritage of the Mediterranean region..

Cagliari Cathedral

The cathedral was built in the 13th century in Pisan-Romanesque style, and it was originally dedicated to Saint Cecilia. It was elevated to cathedral status in 1258. In the 17th and 18th centuries, the cathedral was renovated in Baroque style. In the 1930s, the cathedral received its current façade, which is in Neo-Romanesque style.

The cathedral is a large and imposing building, with a 32-meter-high bell tower. The interior is richly decorated, with a number of Baroque altars and paintings. The cathedral also houses a number of important religious relics, including the skull of Saint Cecilia. There are a number of things to experience at Cagliari Cathedral. Visitors can admire the cathedral's beautiful architecture, both inside and out. They can also visit the cathedral's museum, which houses a collection of religious art and artifacts. The cathedral also offers a number of religious services and events throughout the year.

Admire the cathedral's architecture: The cathedral is a beautiful example of Pisan-Romanesque and Neo-Romanesque architecture. The façade is particularly impressive, with its two bell towers and its rose window.

Visit the cathedral's museum: The cathedral's museum houses a collection of religious art and artifacts, including the skull of Saint Cecilia.

Attend a religious service or event: The cathedral offers a number of religious services and events throughout the year, including Mass, vespers, and concerts.

Take a tour of the cathedral: The cathedral offers guided tours in several languages.

Bastion of Saint Remy

The bastion is located in the Castello district of Cagliari, which is the oldest and most historic part of the city. The staircase leads up to a covered promenade and a large terrace that offers panoramic views of the city and the surrounding area. The terrace is a popular spot for tourists and locals alike, and it is often used for cultural events such as concerts, festivals, and exhibitions.

In addition to its historical and cultural significance, the Bastion of Saint Remy is also a beautiful example of neoclassical architecture. The staircase is made of Pietra Forte, a white and yellow limestone that is quarried in the nearby mountains. The columns and arches of the covered promenade are decorated with elaborate sculptures, and the terrace is lined with palm trees and flowers.

Here are some of the things you can experience at the Bastion of Saint Remy:

- Take in the panoramic views of the city and the surrounding area.
- Visit the covered promenade and admire the neoclassical architecture.
- Attend a cultural event, such as a concert, festival, or exhibition.
- Relax in the shade of the palm trees and enjoy the beautiful scenery.
- Take a walk along the streets of the Castello district and explore the city's history.

Poetto Beach

There are many things to do at Poetto Beach. You can swim, sunbathe, play beach volleyball, or go for a walk along the shore. There are also several restaurants and bars located near the beach, so you can easily get something to eat or drink.

If you are looking for some water sports, there are several companies that offer rentals of kayaks, paddleboards, and other equipment. You can also go sailing, windsurfing, or kitesurfing.

For those who want to explore the surrounding area, there are several hiking trails that lead to viewpoints with stunning views of the beach and the city of Cagliari. You can also visit the Sella del Diavolo, a natural rock formation that offers panoramic views of the area.

Water sports: There are several companies that offer rentals of kayaks, paddleboards, and other equipment. You can also go sailing, windsurfing, or kitesurfing.

Museo Archeologico Nazionale (National Archaeological Museum)

The museum houses finds from the pre-Nuragic and Nuragic age to the Byzantine age, including a large collection of prehistoric bronze statuettes from the Nuragic age, some earlier stone statuettes of female divinities, reconstruction of a Phoenician settlement, the Nora Stone, Carthaginian goldsmith examples, Roman and Italic ceramics and Byzantine jewels.

The museum is located in the Citadel of Museums, a complex of buildings that was once the Royal Arsenal. The museum's exhibits are arranged chronologically, starting with the pre-Nuragic period and ending with the Byzantine era. The highlights of the museum include:

- The Nuragic collection, which is one of the most extensive in the world. The Nuragic people were a Bronze Age culture that inhabited Sardinia from around 1800 to 238 BC. Their culture is characterized by its large stone towers, called nuraghi.

- The Phoenician and Punic collection, which documents the arrival of these cultures to Sardinia in the 8th century BC. The Phoenicians were a Semitic people from the eastern Mediterranean, while the Punic were their descendants. They established a number of trading colonies on Sardinia, which had a significant impact on the island's culture.
- The Roman and Italic collection, which documents the period of Roman rule in Sardinia, which lasted from the 2nd century BC to the 5th century AD. The Romans brought their own culture and technology to Sardinia, which had a profound impact on the island.
- The Byzantine collection, which documents the period of Byzantine rule in Sardinia, which lasted from the 5th to the 11th centuries AD. The Byzantines were a Christian empire that ruled much of the Mediterranean world in the Middle Ages. They brought their own culture and religion to Sardinia, which had a lasting impact on the island.

Molentargius-Saline Regional Park

The park is a popular tourist destination, and there are a number of ways to experience it. Visitors can hike or bike along the trails, take a boat ride on the lake, or visit the Interpretation Center to learn more about the park's flora and fauna.

One of the most popular things to do in the park is to see the flamingos. The flamingos breed in the park from October to April, and they can be seen wading in the shallow waters of the lake. They are a truly stunning sight, and they are sure to leave a lasting impression on any visitor.

Another popular activity in the park is bird watching. There are over 200 species of birds that live in the park, and many of them are easy to spot. Visitors can often see herons, egrets, cormorants, and ducks swimming in the lake, and they may also be lucky enough to see eagles, hawks, and owls.

Castello District

It is located on top of a hill at about 100 meters (328 feet) above sea level, and has always been the place where nobles and rulers used to live and conduct their business. The district is surrounded by medieval walls, and its narrow streets are lined with old buildings, churches, and palaces.

Some of the most popular things to see and do in Castello include:

Visiting the Cathedral of Santa Maria, the main church in Cagliari. The cathedral was built in the 13th century, and its interior is decorated with beautiful paintings and sculptures.
Climbing to the top of Torre di San Pancrazio, a 14th-century tower that offers stunning views of the city and the surrounding area.
Exploring the Citadella dei Musei, a complex of museums that houses the National Archaeological Museum, the Museum of Cinema, and the Museum of Popular Arts and Customs.
Walking through the Bastione di Saint Remy, a 19th-century bastion that now serves as a public park.

San Benedetto Market

The market is divided into two floors. The ground floor is home to the fresh produce section, where you can find a wide variety of fruits, vegetables, meats, cheeses, and other Sardinian specialties. The second floor is dedicated to the fish market, where you can find fresh seafood from all over the Mediterranean.

In addition to the fresh produce and seafood, San Benedetto Market also has a number of other stalls selling prepared foods, souvenirs, and other goods. There are also a number of restaurants and cafes located in the market, where you can enjoy a meal or snack after your shopping.

One of the best things about San Benedetto Market is the atmosphere. The market is always bustling with activity, and the stalls are filled with colorful produce and fresh seafood. The vendors are friendly and welcoming, and they are always happy to offer samples of their wares.

Roman Amphitheatre

It was built in the 2nd century AD and could seat up to 8,000 spectators. The amphitheatre was used for gladiatorial contests, chariot races, animal slaying, and executions. It was also used as a quarry in the Middle Ages and Renaissance.

The amphitheatre is located in the heart of Cagliari, just a short walk from the city center. It is surrounded by a park and is a popular spot for locals and tourists alike. The amphitheatre is well-preserved and you can still see the three levels of seating, the arena, and the tunnels that were used by the gladiators and animals.

There are a few things you can experience at the Roman Amphitheatre of

Cagliari. You can take a guided tour of the site, which will teach you about the history of the amphitheatre and its uses. You can also visit the museum, which houses a collection of artifacts found at the site. And, of course, you can simply wander around the amphitheatre and imagine what it was like to be a spectator at one of the events that took place here

Monte Urpinu Park

It is one of the oldest and largest green lungs of the city, covering an area of 22 hectares. The park is home to a variety of plant and animal life, including pine trees, palm trees, ducks, geese, and rabbits.

The park is a popular spot for locals and tourists alike, and offers a variety of activities to enjoy. Visitors can hike or bike along the park's many trails, have a picnic in one of the many shady areas, or simply relax and enjoy the views. The park also has a playground, a small lake, and a number of fountains.

One of the best things about Monte Urpinu Park is the views. From the top of the park, visitors can see panoramic views of Cagliari, the Mediterranean Sea, and the Stagno di Molentargius nature reserve. On a clear day, it is even possible to see the island of Corsica in the distance.

If you are looking for a peaceful and relaxing place to escape the hustle and bustle of the city, then Monte Urpinu Park is the perfect place for you. The park is a great place to go for a walk, have a picnic, or just relax and enjoy the scenery.

COASTAL GEMS OF SARDINIA

Costa Smeralda

It is known for its white sand beaches, turquoise waters, and luxurious resorts. The area was developed in the 1960s by the Aga Khan, and it quickly became a popular destination for the jet set.

There are many things to experience in Costa Smeralda. Here are a few suggestions:

- Spend a day at the beach. The beaches in Costa Smeralda are some of the most beautiful in the world. They are perfect for swimming, sunbathing, and water sports. Some of the most popular beaches include:

- La Maddalena: This is a long, sandy beach with clear waters. It is a popular spot for families.
- Cala Brandinchi: This is a secluded cove with white sand and turquoise waters. It is a great place to relax and soak up the sun.
- Liscia di Vacca: This is a large beach with golden sand and clear waters. It is a popular spot for water sports.
- .
- Go shopping. There are many luxury boutiques in Costa Smeralda where you can find designer clothes, jewelry, and accessories. There are also a few traditional markets where you can buy souvenirs and local produce.Visit a museum. There are a few museums in Costa Smeralda that showcase the history and culture of the region. The most popular museum is the Museo del Costume, which houses a collection of traditional Sardinian costumes

Porto Cervo

It is located on the Costa Smeralda, which is known for its beautiful beaches, crystal-clear waters, and luxurious resorts. Porto Cervo is a popular destination for celebrities and wealthy individuals, but it is also a great place to visit for anyone who enjoys sunbathing, swimming, sailing, and shopping.

- Go sailing. Porto Cervo is a great place to go sailing. There are many different companies that offer sailing tours and lessons. You can also rent a boat and go sailing on your own.
- Enjoy the nightlife. Porto Cervo has a lively nightlife scene. There are many bars and clubs

that stay open late. You can also find live music and dancing in some of the clubs.

- Visit the beaches. The beaches in Porto Cervo are some of the most beautiful in the world. They are perfect for sunbathing, swimming, and water sports. Some of the most popular beaches include:
- Cala di Volpe
- Liscia Ruja
- La Maddalena

Maddalena Archipelago

The Maddalena Archipelago is a group of 7 major islands and more than 60 smaller ones located in the Tyrrhenian Sea, between Sardinia and Corsica. The archipelago is part of the National Park of the Maddalena Archipelago, which was established in 1994 to protect the islands' unique natural beauty.

The main islands of the archipelago are La Maddalena, Caprera, Budelli, Santa Maria, Spargi, Santo Stefano, and Razzoli. La Maddalena is the largest island and the only one with a town, also called La Maddalena. The other islands are mostly uninhabited or have small fishing villages.

The Maddalena Archipelago is known for its stunning beaches, crystal-clear waters, and rugged cliffs. Some of the most popular beaches include Spiaggia Rosa (Pink Beach) on Budelli Island, Cala Coticcio (Cala Lunga) on Caprera Island, and Cala Sa Conca on Spargi Island.

La Pelosa Beach

La Pelosa is a Blue Flag beach, which means it meets high standards of environmental quality. The sand is soft and fine, and the water is shallow and clear, making it perfect for swimming, sunbathing, and snorkeling. There are also a few small pine trees that provide shade on hot days.

In addition to its natural beauty, La Pelosa Beach is also known for its history. The beach was once the site of a Roman settlement, and there are still some ruins of the settlement visible today. There is also a small lighthouse on the beach that was built in the 1800s.

La Pelosa Beach is a popular destination for both tourists and locals. It can get crowded in the summer months, so it is best to visit early in the day or later in the afternoon. There are a few restaurants and bars near the beach, and there is also a campsite where you can stay if you want to make a longer trip

Cala Luna

It is one of the most popular beaches on the island, and is known for its white sand, clear waters, and towering cliffs. The beach is only accessible by boat or on foot, and the hike down to the beach is steep but rewarding.

Once you reach the beach, you will be able to relax in the sun, swim in the crystal-clear waters, or explore the caves that line the coast. There are also a few restaurants and bars on the beach, so you can grab a bite to eat or a drink.

Stintino

It is located on a promontory that juts out into the Tyrrhenian Sea, and is surrounded by beautiful beaches, including La Pelosa, which is considered to be one of the best beaches in Sardinia.

The town itself is very charming, with whitewashed houses, narrow streets, and a small harbor. There are a few restaurants and shops in Stintino, but it is a relatively quiet town, making it a perfect place to relax and enjoy the scenery.

One of the best things to do in Stintino is to simply relax on one of the beaches. The beaches are all very beautiful, and there is something for everyone, from sandy beaches to rocky coves. If you are looking for something more active, you can go for a swim, go snorkeling or diving, or take a boat trip to explore the surrounding area.

There are also a few historical sites in Stintino, including the ruins of an ancient Roman village and a medieval watchtower. If you are interested in learning more about the history of the area, you can visit the Stintino Museum, which houses a collection of artifacts from the Roman and medieval periods.

Costa Rei

The beaches in Costa Rei are some of the best in Sardinia. They are long and sandy, with shallow waters that are perfect for swimming, sunbathing, and water sports. The water is a beautiful turquoise color, and the sand is so white that it almost glows in the sunlight.

In addition to the beaches, Costa Rei is also home to a number of other natural attractions, including the Capo Ferrato promontory, the Su Gologone waterfall, and the Is Cannoneris nature reserve. The Capo Ferrato promontory is a rocky headland that offers stunning views of the coastline. The Su Gologone waterfall is one of the tallest waterfalls in Sardinia, and it is a popular spot for hiking and swimming. The Is Cannoneris nature reserve is home to a variety of plant and animal life, including the Sardinian deer and the mouflon.

Costa Rei also has a number of historical and cultural attractions. The town of Muravera is home to a number of churches and historical buildings, including the 12th-century San Nicola church. The town of Teulada is also worth visiting, as it is home to the Su Nuraxi di Barumini, a UNESCO World Heritage Site.

Villasimius

It is located on the Gulf of Cagliari, about 60 kilometers from the capital.

The town has a population of around 13,000 people, but it swells to many times that number in the summer months, when it becomes a popular tourist destination.

Villasimius has a long history, dating back to prehistoric times. There are nuraghe (Bronze Age towers) and other archaeological remains in the area. The town was also inhabited by the Phoenicians, Carthaginians, and Romans.

Villasimius is known for its beautiful beaches, which are some of the best in Sardinia. The most popular beaches include Cala Marina, Cala Lunga, and Simius. The town also has a number of other attractions, including a marina, a golf course, and a nature reserve.

In recent years, Villasimius has become a popular destination for windsurfing and kitesurfing. The winds are strong and consistent, making it a perfect place to practice these sports.

Chia

The most famous beach in Chia is Su Giudeu, which is a long stretch of white sand backed by high dunes and juniper trees. The water is crystal clear and turquoise, and the beach is perfect for swimming, sunbathing, and water sports.

Other beaches in the area include Sa Tuerra, Porto Campana, and Cala Cipolla. These beaches are also beautiful, and they offer a variety of different settings. Sa Tuerra is a more secluded beach, while Porto Campana is a popular spot for windsurfing and kitesurfing. Cala Cipolla is a small cove with a sandy beach and clear waters.

In addition to its beaches, Chia also has a number of other attractions. The village itself is small and charming, with a few shops, restaurants, and bars. There is also a 16th-century watchtower, Torre di Chia, which offers stunning views of the surrounding area.

Cala Gonone and the Gulf of Orosei

The beaches in the Gulf of Orosei are all characterized by their white sand, clear waters, and towering cliffs. Cala Luna is the most famous beach in the gulf, and is known for its secluded location and its natural beauty. Cala Mariolu is another popular beach, and is often referred to as the "Pearl of the Gulf". Cala Goloritzé is a more challenging beach to reach, but is worth the effort for its stunning views and dramatic scenery.

In addition to its beautiful beaches, the Gulf of Orosei is also home to a number of other natural attractions, including the Grotta del Bue Marino (Cave of the Sea Cow), a sea cave that is home to a colony of monk seals. The Parco Nazionale del Golfo di Orosei e del Gennargentu (National Park of the Gulf of Orosei and Gennargentu) is a protected area that encompasses the gulf and the surrounding mountains.

.

There are a number of ways to explore the Gulf of Orosei. Boat tours are a popular option, as they allow you to see the beaches and caves from the water. You can also hike to the beaches, or take a boat to Cala Luna and hike to Cala Mariolu

SARDINIAN CUISINE AND LOCAL DELIGHTS

Sardinian Cheese and Pecorino

- **Pecorino Sardo** is a hard, salty cheese with a sharp flavor. It is made from sheep's milk and is aged for at least 6 months. Pecorino Sardo is a Protected Designation of Origin (DOP) product, which means that it must be made according to strict regulations in order to be labeled as such.
- **Fiore Sardo** is another hard sheep's milk cheese, but it is milder and creamier than Pecorino Sardo. It is also a DOP product and is aged for at least 8 months. Fiore Sardo has a nutty flavor and a slightly fruity aroma.

- **Axridda** is a unique Sardinian cheese that is made from sheep's milk and covered in clay. The clay helps to protect the cheese from insects and mold, and it also gives the cheese a distinctive flavor. Axridda is a semi-hard cheese with a salty, tangy flavor.

Seafood and Fish Specialties

- **Bottarga:** is a delicacy made from the dried roe of mullet fish. It is grated over pasta, vegetables, or eaten on its own. Bottarga has a strong, salty flavor, and it is often described as having a briny, nutty taste. It is a popular ingredient in Sardinian cuisine, and it is often used in traditional dishes such as fregola con bottarga and bottarga con pane carasau.

- **Fritto misto:** is a platter of fried seafood, and it is a popular dish in Sardinia. The seafood used in fritto misto varies depending on the season, but it typically includes prawns, squid, anchovies, and other small fish. The seafood is coated in a light batter and then fried until golden brown. Fritto misto is often served with a simple lemon wedge and a side of salad.
- **Burrada:** is a traditional Sardinian dish made with catfish. The catfish is marinated in a vinegar-based sauce and then slowly cooked with walnuts and the liver of the fish. Burrada has a slightly sour flavor, and it is often served as an appetizer. It is a popular dish in the Sardinian capital city of Cagliari, and it is often found on the menus of traditional restaurants.

Sardinian Wine and Vineyards

- **Sella & Mosca** is one of the oldest and most respected wineries in Sardinia. The winery was founded in 1899 by two brothers, Giuseppe and Raimondo Sella, and is located in the town of Alghero. Sella & Mosca is known for its production of Cannonau, a red wine made from the Grenache grape. The winery also produces a number of other wines, including Vermentino, Carignano, and Moscato.

- **Argiolas** is another well-known winery in Sardinia. The winery was founded in 1974 by Gavino Argiolas, and is located in the town of Serdiana. Argiolas is known for its production of high-quality wines, made from a variety of grapes. The winery's most famous wine is the Turriga, a red wine made from the Cannonau grape.

- **Cantina Mesa** is a newer winery in Sardinia, founded in 1998. The winery is located in the town of Sant'Anna Arresi, in the south of the island. Cantina Mesa is known for its production of Vermentino, a white wine made from the Vermentino grape. The winery's Vermentino di Gallura is one of the most highly-rated wines in Sardinia.

Pane Carasau (Sardinian Flatbread)

- **Pane carasau:** This is the most common type of pane carasau. It is made with a simple dough and is cooked until it is very thin and crispy. Pane carasau is often eaten as a snack or appetizer, or it can be used to make sandwiches or wraps.
- **Pane guttiau:** This type of pane carasau is even thinner than pane carasau. It is made with a more delicate dough and is cooked until it is very fragile. Pane guttiau is often eaten with cheese, salami, or other savory toppings.

- **Pane frattau:** This dish is made with pane carasau that is soaked in broth, topped with tomato sauce, cheese, and a poached egg. Pane frattau is a traditional Sardinian dish that is often served for breakfast or lunch.

NATURAL BEAUTY AND OUTDOOR ACTIVITIES

Gola di Gorropu Gorge

It is one of the deepest canyons in Europe, reaching a depth of over 500 meters (1,640 feet). The gorge is also one of the longest in Sardinia, stretching for over 15 kilometers (9.3 miles).

The top 3 things to do in Gola di Gorropu Gorge are:

- **Hiking:** The most popular activity in the gorge is hiking. There are several trails that lead through the gorge, ranging from easy to challenging. The most popular trail is the Sentiero Selvaggio 4, which is a 7-hour hike that takes hikers to the bottom of the gorge.

- **Canyoning:** Canyoning is another popular activity in the gorge. This involves rappelling, swimming, and jumping down waterfalls. There are several companies that offer canyoning tours in the gorge.
- **Birdwatching:** The gorge is home to a variety of birds, including eagles, hawks, and falcons. Birdwatchers can spot these birds from the rim of the gorge or from the bottom of the gorge.

Monte Tiscali

It is home to a unique archaeological site, the Nuragic village of Tiscali. The village is located in a sinkhole, or dolina, in the side of the mountain. The houses are built into the rock walls of the dolina, and there is a natural spring that provides water. The village was inhabited from the 15th to the 8th centuries BC, and it is one of the best-preserved Nuragic villages in Sardinia.

The top 3 things to do at Monte Tiscali are:

- **Visit the Nuragic village.** This is the main attraction at Monte Tiscali, and it is well worth the hike to get there. The village is made up of a number of round houses, as well as a nuraghe, or tower. There are also a number of other prehistoric structures in the area, including a sacred well and a menhir.

- **Go hiking.** There are a number of hiking trails in the area around Monte Tiscali. The most popular trail is the one that leads to the village, but there are also trails that go to other viewpoints and natural features.
- **Enjoy the scenery.** The scenery around Monte Tiscali is stunning. The mountains are covered in lush vegetation, and there are a number of waterfalls and streams. The views from the top of the mountain are simply amazing.

Asinara National Park

It is home to a variety of wildlife, including wild donkeys, mouflon, and many species of birds. The park is also known for its beautiful beaches, pristine waters, and stunning scenery.

Here are the top 3 attractions in Asinara National Park:

- **Fornelli:** This is a small village located in the north of the park. It is home to a few traditional houses and a small church. Fornelli is a great place to start your exploration of the park, as it is well-connected to the other attractions.
- **Cala Reale:** This is a beautiful beach located in the south of the park. It is known for its white

sand, clear waters, and secluded location. Cala Reale is a great place to relax and enjoy the natural beauty of the park.

- **Punta Scornosa:** This is a rocky promontory located in the west of the park. It offers stunning views of the surrounding coastline. Punta Scornosa is a great place to go for a hike or simply enjoy the scenery.

Gennargentu National Park

It is the largest national park in Sardinia, covering an area of over 74,000 hectares. The park is home to a variety of different landscapes, including mountains, forests, valleys, and rivers.

The highest peak in the park is Punta La Marmora, which is 1,834 meters (6,017 feet) tall. Other notable peaks include Monte Linas, Monte

Tiscali, and Monte Corrasi. The park is also home to a variety of different plant and animal life, including cork oaks, juniper trees, wild boars, deers, and wolves.

There are a number of different hiking trails in the park, ranging from easy to challenging. Some of the most popular trails include the Selvaggio Blu, which is a 5-day trek that takes hikers through some of the most remote and wild parts of the park. The park is also home to a number of archaeological sites, including the Nuraghe Tiscali, which is a well-preserved nuragic village that dates back to the Bronze Age.

Supramonte Mountains

They are the highest mountains on the island, with their highest peak, Punta La Marmora, reaching an elevation of 1,834 meters (6,017 feet). The Supramonte Mountains are a popular destination for hiking, mountaineering, and camping.

The Supramonte Mountains are made up of limestone and dolomite rock, which has been eroded over time to form a variety of stunning landscapes. These include deep gorges, towering cliffs, and lush valleys. The mountains are also home to a variety of plant and animal life, including forests of cork oaks, holm oaks, and junipers.

One of the most popular hiking trails in the Supramonte Mountains is the Selvaggio Blu, which is a 170-kilometer (106-mile) trek that takes hikers through some of the most remote and beautiful parts of the range. The trail is challenging, but it offers stunning views of the mountains and the surrounding countryside. Another popular destination in the Supramonte Mountains is the Gola Su Gorropu, which is a deep gorge that is over 1,000 meters (3,300 feet) deep. The gorge is home to a variety of wildlife, including wild boars, eagles, and falcons.

Capo Testa

Capo Testa is a small peninsula (actually an island, then artificially connected to the mainland) located in the north of Sardinia, a few kilometers from Santa Teresa di Gallura. It is a popular tourist destination, known for its beautiful beaches, dramatic rock formations, and hiking trails. The peninsula is made up of granite rock, which has been eroded by the wind and sea over time, creating a variety of shapes and formations. Some of the most popular rock formations include the "Elephant Rock," the "Heart Rock," and the "Mushroom Rock."

There are several beaches on Capo Testa, each with its own unique character. The most popular beach is Cala Longa, a long, sandy beach with calm waters. Other beaches include Cala Marina, Cala Brandinchi, and Cala Spinosa.

In addition to its beaches, Capo Testa is also home to a number of hiking trails. The most popular trail is the Sentiero del Faro, which leads to the Capo Testa lighthouse. The lighthouse is located on a cliff overlooking the sea, and offers stunning views of the surrounding area

Isola dell'Asinara

Isola dell'Asinara is a small island off the northwestern coast of Sardinia. It is known for its wild and unspoiled nature, which has been protected as a national park since 1997. The island is home to a variety of wildlife, including wild horses, donkeys, mouflon, and many species of birds. The waters around the island are also home to a rich marine life, making it a popular destination for scuba diving and snorkeling.

The island has a long and varied history. It was once inhabited by the Nuragic people, who built several nuraghi, or ancient stone towers, on the island. In the Middle Ages, the island was used as a prison for political dissidents. In the 20th century, it was used as a military base and a leper colony.

Today, Isola dell'Asinara is a popular tourist destination. Visitors can enjoy hiking, biking, swimming, and sunbathing on the island's many beautiful beaches. There are also several museums and historical sites on the island that can be visited.

Nuragic Sites

The Nuragic civilization is one of the most fascinating and mysterious in the Mediterranean. Flourishing on the island of Sardinia from the Bronze Age to the Roman period, the Nuragic people left behind a vast network of megalithic structures, including nuraghi, tholos tombs, and sacred wells.

The nuraghe is the most iconic symbol of the Nuragic civilization. These massive stone towers were built with a corbeled technique, in which each course of stones projects slightly inward, creating a dome-shaped roof. Nuraghi could be single towers or complex structures with multiple towers, courtyards, and stairways. They served as fortresses, granaries, and religious centers.
The most famous nuraghe is Su Nuraxi di Barumini, which is a UNESCO World Heritage Site. This massive complex is made up of six towers and a surrounding wall. It is thought to have been built in the 16th century BC and was once the center of a large Nuragic settlement.

Su Gorropu Canyon

It is a deep gorge that is over 500 meters (1,640 feet) at its deepest point, and it is flanked by limestone walls that rise up to 1,500 meters (4,920 feet) high. The canyon is located in the Supramonte region of Sardinia, and it is a popular destination for hikers, climbers, and photographers.

The best time to visit Su Gorropu Canyon is from

September to April, when the weather is mild and the temperatures are not too hot. The canyon can be accessed via a number of trails, but the most popular one is the Sa Barca Bridge trail. This trail begins in the town of Dorgali, and it takes about 4-5 hours to hike to the canyon.

Once you reach the canyon, you can explore it on foot or by climbing. There are a number of different trails that you can take, and you can also stop to admire the stunning views of the canyon walls. If you are feeling adventurous, you can also try canyoning, which is a type of adventure sport that involves hiking, swimming, and rappelling through the canyon.

Is Zuddas Caves

They are part of an underground cavity complex that passes through Mount Meana, a 240-meter-high hill. The tourist route inside the cave is about half a kilometer long, and passes through stalactites, stalagmites and impressive formations similar to petrified waterfalls.

The name Is Zuddas means "the needles" in the local dialect, and refers to the aragonite needles that can be found inside the cave. These needles are a type of mineral that is formed when water seeps through the limestone and evaporates, leaving behind the aragonite crystals.

The Is Zuddas Caves are home to a variety of other

interesting formations, including stalactites, stalagmites, flowstones, and helictites. Helictites are a type of stalactite that grows in a spiral pattern, and their formation is still not fully understood by scientists.

CULTURAL EXPERIENCES IN SARDINIA

Nuraghe Su Nuraxi

The site consists of a central tower, surrounded by four smaller towers and a curtain wall. The central tower is 18.6 meters high and has three superimposed chambers. The smaller towers are all connected to each other by a system of corridors and stairways. The complex is also surrounded by a large village, which was inhabited from the 13th to the 6th centuries BC.

The nuraghe was built in the late Bronze Age, and was

probably used as a defensive stronghold. However, it is also possible that it had religious or ceremonial functions. The site was abandoned in the Iron Age, but it was rediscovered in the 19th century.

Su Nuraxi is a fascinating example of the nuragic civilization, which flourished in Sardinia from the 19th to the 7th centuries BC. The nuragic people were a skilled and sophisticated culture, and their architecture is a testament to their ingenuity.

Museo del Costume (Costume Museum)

The museum was founded in 1976 and is located in a beautiful building designed by the architect Antonio Simon Mossa. The collection includes over 8,000 items, dating from the 18th to the early 20th centuries. The costumes are displayed in chronological order, and each one is accompanied by a detailed label that describes its provenance, materials, and construction.

The museum's collection is divided into several sections, each of which focuses on a different aspect of Sardinian culture. The section on costumes includes examples of traditional dress from all over the island, as well as a variety of accessories, such as jewelry, hats, and shoes. The section on textiles features a collection of Sardinian fabrics, including wool, linen, and silk. The section on tools and objects of everyday use includes items such as agricultural tools, household utensils, and musical instruments.

Sardinian Folk Festivals

- **Sant'Efisio Procession:** This is one of the most important religious festivals in Sardinia, and it takes place in Cagliari every year in May. The procession honors the martyr Saint Efisio, and it features a large statue of the saint being carried through the streets of the city.
- **La Cavalcata Sarda:** This is a traditional horseback festival that takes place in Sassari every year in August. The festival features hundreds of horsemen dressed in traditional Sardinian costumes, and it is a colorful and exciting spectacle.
- Sagra del Redentore: This is a summer festival that takes place in Nuoro every year in July. The festival features traditional Sardinian dances, music, and food, and it is a great way to experience the culture of the island.

- **Sa Sartiglia:** This is a traditional horse race that takes place in Oristano every year in February. The race is full of excitement and pageantry, and it is a must-see for any visitor to Sardinia.
- **Autunno in Barbagia:** This is a fall festival that takes place in various towns in the Barbagia region of Sardinia every year in October. The festival features traditional Sardinian dances, music, and food, and it is a great way to experience the culture of the island.

Sant'Antioco Island

Sant'Antioco Island is a beautiful island located off the southwest coast of Sardinia. It is the second largest island in the Sardinian region, after Sardinia itself, and is home to a rich history and culture.

The island was first inhabited by the Phoenicians in the 8th century BC, and later by the Romans, Carthaginians, and Byzantines. In the Middle Ages, Sant'Antioco was an important commercial center, and its salt mines were renowned throughout the Mediterranean.

Today, Sant'Antioco is a popular tourist destination, thanks to its beautiful beaches, charming villages, and fascinating historical sites. Some of the most popular attractions on the island include:

The Basilica of Sant'Antioco Martire, which is a 12th-century church that houses the remains of the island's patron saint.
The Catacombs of Sant'Antioco, which are a network of underground tunnels that were used as a cemetery by Christians in the 2nd-7th centuries AD.
The Roman ruins of Sulci, which were once a major city in the Roman Empire.
The beaches of Cala Marina, Cala Lunga, and Cala Cipolla, which are some of the most beautiful beaches in Sardinia.

Carloforte - Tabarka

It was founded in 1738 by a group of Ligurian fishermen who were expelled from Tabarka, a Tunisian island that they had colonized in the 16th century. The inhabitants of Carloforte still speak a dialect of Ligurian, and the town has a strong Ligurian cultural identity.

The town is located on a promontory overlooking the sea. The old town is walled, and the streets are narrow and winding. The main square, Piazza Repubblica, is home to the town hall and the church of San Carlo Borromeo. Other notable landmarks include the Tower of San Vittorio, the Mura di Cinta (city walls), and the Museo del Mare (Maritime Museum).

Tharros Archaeological Site

The site is home to the ruins of a settlement that was founded in the 8th century BC by the Phoenicians and later became an important Roman city. Tharros was abandoned in the 11th century AD, but its ruins remain a popular tourist destination.

The archaeological site at Tharros is divided into two main areas: the residential area and the necropolis. The residential area is home to the remains of temples, baths, houses, and shops. The necropolis is located to the north and south of the residential area and contains the remains of thousands of graves.

Some of the most notable structures at Tharros include

the Tophet, a Phoenician sanctuary dedicated to the worship of the god Baal Hammon; the Roman baths, which are well-preserved and still contain some of their original mosaics; and the Temple of Athena, which was one of the largest temples in Sardinia.

Orgosolo Murals

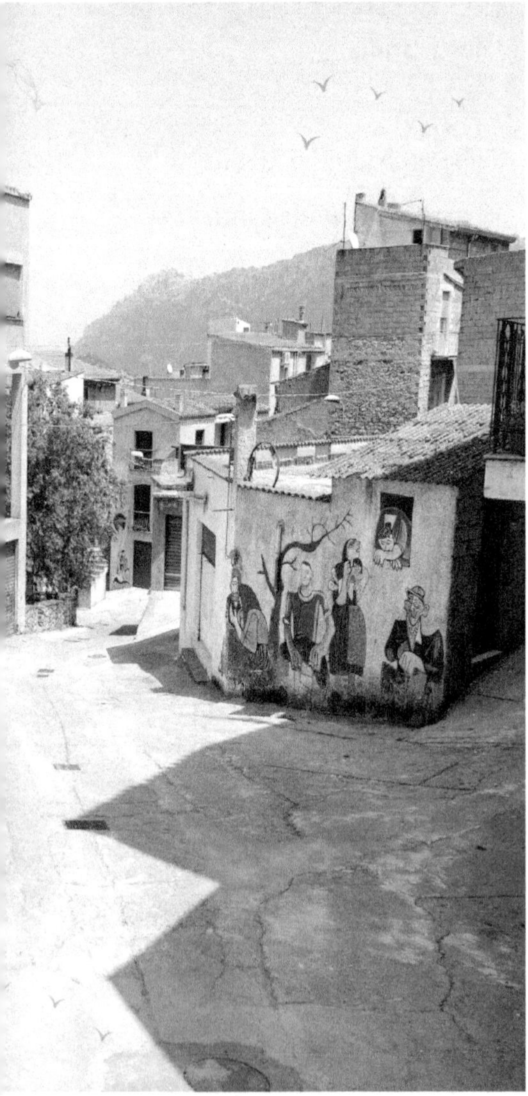

The Orgosolo Murals are a collection of over 150 murals that decorate the streets of Orgosolo, a small town in the Barbagia region of Sardinia. The murals cover a wide range of topics, from political and social commentary to traditional Sardinian culture.

The first murals in Orgosolo were painted in the late 1960s by a group of anarchists who wanted to use art as a way to express their political views. These early murals were often quite political, and they often depicted scenes of violence and oppression. In the 1970s, the murals began to take on a more social focus, and they often depicted scenes of everyday life in Orgosolo.

In the 1980s, the murals began to attract the attention of international artists, and many foreign artists began to come to Orgosolo to paint murals. This led to a diversification of the murals, and they began to cover a wider range of topics. Today, the murals of Orgosolo are a popular tourist destination, and they are seen as a symbol of the town's cultural and political identity.

Some of the most famous murals in Orgosolo include:

- "The Bandit" (1969), which depicts a masked bandit with a gun in his hand.
- "The Pratobello Revolution" (1975), which commemorates the local uprising against the Italian government's plans to build a military base in the area.
- "The World's Prisoners" (1980), which depicts a group of people from different countries who are all imprisoned.

- "The Global Village" (1990), which depicts a group of people from different cultures who are all living together in peace

Giants of Mont'e Prama

The Giants of Mont'e Prama are a group of ancient stone sculptures created by the Nuragic civilization of Sardinia. Fragmented into numerous pieces, they were discovered in March 1974 on farmland near Mont'e Prama, in the comune of Cabras, province of Oristano, in central-western Sardinia. The statues are carved in local sandstone and their height varies between 2 and 2.5 meters.

The sculptures represent warriors, archers, and boxers, and are thought to date back to the 13th–9th century BC. They are some of the largest and most elaborate sculptures ever found from the Nuragic period, and their discovery has shed new light on this mysterious culture.

The Giants of Mont'e Prama were originally found in a necropolis, or burial ground, suggesting that they may have been used as funerary monuments. However, their exact purpose is still unknown. Some scholars believe that they may have been used as cult statues, while others believe that they may have been simply decorative.

Sardinian Handicrafts and Artisan Workshops

Sardinia is a land of ancient traditions, and this is reflected in its rich handicrafts. From the intricate filigree jewelry of the Barbagia region to the colorful weavings of the Marghine, there is a wide variety of crafts to be found on the island.

One of the most popular handicrafts in Sardinia is filigree. This delicate art form involves the weaving of silver or gold wire into intricate patterns. Filigree jewelry is often made in the shapes of flowers, animals, or religious symbols. It is a highly skilled craft, and many of the filigree workshops in Sardinia have been passed down through generations of families.

Another popular handicraft in Sardinia is weaving. The island is home to a number of different weaving traditions, each with its own unique style. The Marghine region is known for its colorful woolen rugs and blankets, while the Nuoro region is known for its intricate basketwork.

Sardinian Language and Traditions

One of the most distinctive aspects of Sardinian culture is its language, Sardinian. Sardinian is a Romance language, but it is quite different from Italian. It has its own unique vocabulary, grammar, and pronunciation.

There are many different dialects of Sardinian, and each dialect is spoken in a different part of the island. The most common dialect is Campidanese, which is spoken in the central part of Sardinia. Other major dialects include Logudorese, spoken in the north, and Barbagia, spoken in the east. Sardinian is a very old language, and it has been influenced by many different cultures over the centuries. The Romans brought Latin to Sardinia, and the language has also been influenced by Arabic, Spanish, and Catalan. This rich linguistic heritage has given Sardinian a unique character.

Sardinian is not an official language of Italy, but it is still widely spoken on the island. About 40% of Sardinians speak Sardinian as their first language, and another 30% speak it as a second language. Sardinian is also taught in schools on the island.

DAY TRIPS AND EXCURSIONS IN SARDINIA

Alghero and Neptune's Grotto

Morning:

- Start your day by traveling to Alghero, located on the northwestern coast of Sardinia. You can reach Alghero by bus or car from nearby cities like Cagliari or Sassari. Enjoy the scenic journey as you drive along the picturesque coastline, offering glimpses of crystal-clear turquoise waters.
- Upon arrival in Alghero, take a leisurely stroll

along the captivating cobblestone streets of the historic city center. Marvel at the well-preserved medieval walls, which encircle the charming old town. Explore the bustling harbor area and indulge in some shopping for local crafts, souvenirs, and delectable Sardinian specialties.

Lunch:

- As noon approaches, savor a delicious lunch at one of the traditional restaurants in Alghero. Taste the authentic flavors of Sardinian cuisine, including fresh seafood dishes like "spaghetti alla bottarga" or "fregola con arselle." Accompany your meal with a glass of local Vermentino wine, renowned for its crispness and aromatic qualities.

- **Afternoon:**
- Following lunch, embark on an unforgettable boat trip to Neptune's Grotto (Grotta di Nettuno), located on the mesmerizing Capo Caccia promontory. Hop aboard a boat at the Alghero harbor and enjoy a scenic ride along the breathtaking coastline. Marvel at the rugged cliffs and the azure waters of the Mediterranean Sea.
- Upon arrival at Neptune's Grotto, prepare to be amazed by the natural wonders within. Follow a guided tour through the stunning caves, adorned with impressive stalactites and stalagmites that have formed over thousands of years. Marvel at the breathtaking underground lake and listen to fascinating stories and legends surrounding this mystical place.

Expenses:

- **Transportation:** The cost of transportation will depend on your starting location and chosen mode of transport. Estimate around €20-30 for a round-trip bus ticket from Cagliari or Sassari.

- **Lunch:** Expect to spend around €20-30 per person for a satisfying meal at a local restaurant.
- **Boat trip to Neptune's Grotto:** Prices for boat tours to Neptune's Grotto can vary, but anticipate spending approximately €15-20 per person for the round-trip boat ride and entrance fee to the caves.
- **Note:** The expenses mentioned are approximate and may vary based on personal preferences and seasonal variations.

Bosa and the Temo River

Morning:

- Begin your day with a delightful breakfast at one of Bosa's cozy cafes, savoring freshly brewed Italian coffee and traditional pastries. Afterward, set off on a stroll along the picturesque streets of

Bosa's Old Town, marveling at its colorful houses and quaint alleys. Make your way to the Malaspina Castle, a medieval fortress perched on a hilltop, offering panoramic views of the town and the surrounding landscape.

Mid-Morning:

- Next, head towards the Temo River, the only navigable river in Sardinia. Rent a boat or join a guided river tour to explore its tranquil waters. Drift along the riverbanks, admiring the lush vegetation, ancient bridges, and the charming facades of riverside buildings. Capture the beauty of Bosa from a unique perspective as you glide through the crystal-clear waters.

Lunchtime:

- After working up an appetite, relish a scrumptious seafood lunch at one of the waterfront restaurants overlooking the Temo River. Indulge in local specialties such as fregola con arselle (Sardinian couscous with clams) or freshly grilled fish, accompanied by a glass of renowned Sardinian wine.

Afternoon:

- Spend the afternoon exploring Bosa's cultural treasures. Visit the Cathedral of Bosa, an architectural masterpiece with its distinctive pink facade and stunning interior. Wander through the narrow streets lined with artisan shops and boutiques, where you can find unique handcrafted items and souvenirs.

Late Afternoon:

- As the day winds down, make your way back to

the Temo River for a leisurely stroll along the riverside promenade. Admire the vibrant sunset casting a warm glow over the river, creating a magical ambiance. Stop by the charming Ponte Vecchio, an ancient bridge that spans the Temo River, and capture some memorable photos.

Evening:

- Wrap up your day trip with a delightful dinner at a traditional Sardinian trattoria. Relish the flavors of Sardinian cuisine, such as malloreddus pasta with sausage ragu or seadas, a sweet fried pastry filled with cheese and drizzled with honey. Toast to a remarkable day in Bosa with a glass of mirto, a traditional Sardinian liqueur.

Expenses (estimated):

- Breakfast: €8-12
- Boat rental or guided river tour: €25-50 per person
- Lunch at a waterfront restaurant: €20-35 per person
- Cathedral of Bosa entrance fee: €3-5
- Souvenirs and shopping: variable
- Dinner at a trattoria: €25-40 per person

Tavolara Island

9:00 AM: Departure from the Port of Olbia

- Kickstart your Tavolara Island day trip by heading to the Port of Olbia, located on the northeastern coast of Sardinia. Board a comfortable ferry or boat that will take you on a scenic journey towards the stunning Tavolara Island.

10:00 AM: Arrival at Tavolara Island

- After an hour-long boat ride, you'll arrive at Tavolara Island, a hidden gem nestled in the crystal-clear waters of the Tyrrhenian Sea. As you step onto the island, you'll be greeted by breathtaking panoramic views and a sense of tranquility.

10:30 AM: Hiking to the Summit

- Embark on an exhilarating hike to the summit of Tavolara Island. The trail offers mesmerizing views of the surrounding turquoise sea and the rugged coastline. As you ascend, take in the fragrant Mediterranean vegetation and keep an eye out for unique bird species that call the island home.

12:30 PM: Picnic Lunch with Scenic Views

- Find a cozy spot overlooking the sea and indulge in a delightful picnic lunch. Savor the flavors of local Sardinian cuisine, including fresh seafood, traditional cheeses, and crusty bread. Take your time to relax, unwind, and absorb the serenity of this idyllic setting.

2:00 PM: Beach Exploration and Snorkeling

- Make your way to Tavolara's pristine beaches, renowned for their soft white sands and inviting azure waters. Spend the afternoon sunbathing, swimming, or snorkeling in the abundant marine life-filled waters. Discover colorful coral reefs and encounter schools of vibrant fish as you explore the underwater world.

4:00 PM: Visit the Village of Tavolara

- Take a leisurely stroll to the charming village of Tavolara, located at the base of the island. Immerse yourself in the island's rich history and culture as you wander through the narrow streets lined with colorful houses and quaint shops. Don't forget to visit the local cafes and try some authentic Sardinian gelato.

6:00 PM: Departure from Tavolara Island

- Reluctantly bid farewell to Tavolara Island as you board the boat back to the Port of Olbia. Reflect on the unforgettable experiences and memories created during your day trip.

Expenses:

- Ferry or boat ticket: Approximately €20-30 per person (round trip)
- Picnic lunch: €15-20 per person (including local specialties and drinks)
- Snorkeling equipment rental: €10-15 per person (optional)
- Souvenirs and local products: Budget depending on personal preference

Grotta di Nettuno (Neptune's Cave)

Morning:

- We begin our day trip by departing from the charming town of Alghero, where we will meet our experienced guide and hop on a comfortable coach. As we drive along the picturesque coastline, the sparkling turquoise waters of the Mediterranean Sea will captivate your senses.

- Upon arrival at the entrance of Neptune's Cave, we will descend a scenic stairway carved into the cliffs, offering panoramic views of the surrounding cliffs and sea. The cave's grandeur will unfold before your eyes as we enter its mystical chambers adorned with awe-inspiring stalactites and stalagmites, illuminated by soft lighting.

Afternoon:

- Following our cave exploration, we will head to a nearby coastal village, where a delicious traditional Sardinian lunch awaits us. Indulge in local delicacies, such as fresh seafood, pasta dishes, and delightful regional desserts, all accompanied by a glass of the island's renowned Vermentino wine.

- With our appetites sated, we'll have the opportunity to stroll along the village's charming streets, browse local boutiques, or relax on the golden sandy beaches. You can also opt to take a refreshing dip in the crystal-clear waters of the Mediterranean, embracing the tranquility of the surroundings.

Evening:

- As the day draws to a close, we will board our coach and return to Alghero, reflecting on the incredible experiences and memories made throughout the day. The journey back will provide us with a final chance to admire Sardinia's rugged coastline and vibrant sunset, creating a lasting impression of this enchanting island.

Expenses:

The day trip to Neptune's Cave in Sardinia costs approximately $100 per person, including transportation, guided tour, entrance fees to the cave, and a traditional Sardinian lunch. Additional expenses may include souvenirs, personal shopping, or any optional activities you choose to participate in during your free time.

Costa Verde and the Sand Dunes

Morning:

- 8:00 AM: Depart from your accommodation in Cagliari and head towards Costa Verde, located on the island's western coast. It's approximately a 90-minute drive.
- 9:30 AM: Arrive at the Costa Verde region and visit the charming mining town of Ingurtosu. Explore the

remnants of the mining industry, which was once the economic backbone of the area.

- 11:00 AM: Continue your journey to Piscinas, where you'll find the awe-inspiring sand dunes of Sardinia. Prepare to be amazed by the dramatic landscape and the golden sands stretching as far as the eye can see.

Afternoon:

- 12:30 PM: Enjoy a picnic lunch amidst the dunes, surrounded by nature's tranquility. Savor local delicacies like pane carasau (traditional Sardinian flatbread) and pecorino cheese, paired with a glass of Vermentino wine.
- 2:00 PM: Take a leisurely stroll along the dunes, capturing stunning photographs of this unique natural wonder. Bask in the peaceful ambiance and the panoramic views of the sparkling Mediterranean Sea.

- 3:30 PM: Head towards the nearby beach of Scivu for a refreshing dip in the crystal-clear waters or sunbathe on the pristine sandy shoreline.

Evening:

- 6:00 PM: Bid farewell to Costa Verde and start your journey back to Cagliari.
- 7:30 PM: Arrive in Cagliari, where you can indulge in a delicious dinner at one of the local restaurants, trying Sardinian specialties such as malloreddus (Sardinian pasta) with tomato sauce and saffron-infused bottarga.

Expenses:

- Car rental: Approximately €50 for the day.
- Gasoline: Approximately €20 for a round trip.
- Picnic lunch: Around €15 per person, including local products and wine.
- Beach facilities (optional): Umbrella and sunbed rental for €10-15.

Oristano and the Sinis Peninsula

9:00 AM - Depart from Cagliari to Oristano

- Take the early morning bus from Cagliari to Oristano, a scenic journey that takes approximately 1.5 hours.

10:30 AM - Explore Oristano

- Arrive in Oristano and start your day by exploring this charming city. Visit the historic center and discover its beautiful architecture, including the iconic Torre di San Cristoforo.
- Take a stroll along the Corso Umberto I, the main street lined with shops, cafes, and restaurants.
- Don't miss the chance to sample some traditional Sardinian cuisine for lunch at a local restaurant.

1:30 PM - Visit the Sinis Peninsula

- Take a local bus from Oristano to the Sinis Peninsula, a journey that lasts around 30 minutes.
- Arrive at the stunning coastline and visit the archaeological site of Tharros, an ancient Phoenician city with well-preserved ruins. Marvel at the ancient Roman amphitheater and the remains of ancient temples.

3:30 PM - Enjoy the Beaches and Nature

- Take some time to relax and enjoy the beautiful beaches of the Sinis Peninsula. The area is known for its crystal-clear waters and pristine white sand. You can also take a refreshing swim if the weather permits.
- Consider joining a boat tour around the Mal di Ventre Island to explore the coastal beauty and spot marine wildlife.

6:00 PM - Return to Oristano and Depart for Cagliari

- Take the local bus back to Oristano.
- Board the bus back to Cagliari, reflecting on the wonderful day you've had exploring Oristano and the Sinis Peninsula.

8:00 PM - Arrive in Cagliari

- Return to Cagliari, marking the end of your day trip to Oristano and the Sinis Peninsula in Sardinia.

Expenses

Transportation:

- Roundtrip bus ticket from Cagliari to Oristano: €20
- Local bus ticket from Oristano to Sinis Peninsula: €5

Activities:

- Entrance fee to Tharros archaeological site: €5
- Optional boat tour around the Mal di Ventre Island: €25

Food:

- Lunch at a local restaurant in Oristano or the Sinis Peninsula: €15
- Snacks and drinks throughout the day: €10

Total estimated expenses: €80

Barumini - Su Nuraxi Archaeological Site

Morning:

- Start your day early with a hearty breakfast at your hotel in Cagliari, the capital city of Sardinia. Afterward, hop into a rental car or join a guided tour to make your way to the town of Barumini, approximately 60 kilometers north of Cagliari. The scenic drive through the Sardinian countryside sets the mood for an exciting adventure.
- Arriving in Barumini, head straight to the Su Nuraxi Archaeological Site. This remarkable archaeological complex dates back to the 16th century BC and showcases the Bronze Age civilization of the

Nuragic people. Explore the well-preserved nuraghe, a distinctive stone tower, and its surrounding village. Immerse yourself in the mysteries of this ancient civilization as you wander through the complex and learn about their way of life.

Afternoon:

- As midday approaches, take a break from the exploration and enjoy a traditional Sardinian lunch at a local trattoria. Indulge in authentic dishes such as malloreddus pasta with saffron, roasted suckling pig, and a selection of local cheeses. Savor the flavors of Sardinian cuisine and recharge for the rest of your adventure.
- Once you've satisfied your appetite, continue your journey to the nearby Giara di Gesturi. This nature reserve is renowned for its unique landscape and the presence of wild horses, known as the Giara horses. Take a leisurely walk along the trails, marvel at the vast plateau, and keep an eye out for these beautiful creatures in their natural habitat.

Evening:

- As the sun starts to set, make your way back to Cagliari, reflecting on the day's discoveries and experiences. Consider stopping by a local winery on your return journey to savor some of Sardinia's renowned wines.

Expenses:

- Rental car or guided tour: Prices vary depending on the chosen option. Expect to spend around €50-€100 for transportation.
- Su Nuraxi Archaeological Site entrance fee: €10 per person.
- Lunch at a local trattoria: Budget around €20-€30 per person.
- Optional visit to a winery: Tastings typically range from €15-€30 per person.

Castelsardo

Morning:

- 9:00 AM: Start your day with a leisurely breakfast at a local café. Enjoy a traditional Sardinian pastry, such as a seada or a pardulas, accompanied by a strong espresso.
- 10:00 AM: Head to Castelsardo's historic center. Explore the narrow cobblestone streets and marvel at the medieval architecture. Visit the striking Castello dei Doria, a fortress perched atop a rocky promontory, offering panoramic views of the Gulf of Asinara.
- 11:30 AM: Immerse yourself in the local culture by visiting the Museo dell'Intreccio

Mediterraneo, a museum dedicated to traditional basket weaving. Witness skilled artisans at work and admire the intricate designs.

Afternoon:

- 1:00 PM: Indulge in a delicious lunch at a local trattoria. Savor the flavors of Sardinian cuisine, such as culurgiones (stuffed pasta), fregola (a type of pasta), or succulent seafood dishes. Expect to spend around 30-40 euros per person for a satisfying meal.
- 2:30 PM: Make your way to Lu Bagnu, a beautiful beach just outside Castelsardo. Relax on the sandy shore, take a dip in the crystal-clear waters, or simply bask in the Mediterranean sunshine. Don't forget to bring

your beach essentials, including sunscreen and a beach towel.

- 4:30 PM: Return to Castelsardo and explore the charming shops that line the streets. Browse local handicrafts, including ceramics, textiles, and jewelry. Purchase unique souvenirs to commemorate your visit.

Evening:

- 6:00 PM: End your day trip with a visit to the Cattedrale di Sant'Antonio Abate. Admire the impressive architecture and stunning views from the church's terrace. If you're lucky, you might catch a beautiful sunset over the sea.
- 7:30 PM: Treat yourself to a delightful dinner at a waterfront restaurant. Sample the island's specialties, such as bottarga (cured fish roe), porceddu (roast suckling pig), or a refreshing seafood risotto. Plan to spend around 40-50 euros per

person for a memorable dining experience.

- 9:00 PM: Before leaving Castelsardo, take a leisurely stroll along the harbor promenade, soaking up the enchanting atmosphere of this coastal town. Capture some photos and relish the memories of your unforgettable day in Sardinia.

Expenses (approximate):

- Breakfast: 5-10 euros
- Museum admission: 5 euros
- Lunch: 30-40 euros
- Beach essentials: Personal
- Shopping: Personal
- Dinner: 40-50 euros

Porto Flavia

9:00 AM - Departure from Cagliari

- Start your day early by departing from the vibrant city of Cagliari towards the scenic Costa Verde region. You can choose to rent a car or join a guided tour for a hassle-free experience. The journey takes approximately 1.5 hours, allowing you to soak in the beautiful Sardinian landscapes along the way.

10:30 AM - Arrival at Porto Flavia

- Upon reaching Porto Flavia, prepare to be mesmerized by its unique beauty. Porto Flavia is an awe-inspiring sea harbor situated on the southwestern coast of Sardinia. It was once a bustling mining port and is now a remarkable historical site. Explore the dramatic cliffs, ancient tunnels, and breathtaking sea views. Take your time to learn about the rich mining history and the engineering marvel that is Porto Flavia.

12:30 PM - Lunch by the Sea

- After immersing yourself in the wonders of Porto Flavia, enjoy a delightful lunch by the sea. There are several charming restaurants and trattorias nearby that offer traditional Sardinian cuisine. Sample delicious seafood dishes, such as fresh fish, pasta with bottarga (Sardinian caviar), and local specialties like malloreddus (Sardinian gnocchi). Indulge in the rich flavors of the Mediterranean while taking in the picturesque coastal scenery.

2:00 PM - Beach Time at Portixeddu

- After a satisfying meal, head to the nearby Portixeddu beach for some relaxation and sun-soaked moments. This sandy paradise boasts crystal-clear waters and stunning vistas. Unwind on the beach, swim in the azure sea, or simply soak up the sun. Take a leisurely stroll along the shore and enjoy the tranquility of this hidden gem.

5:00 PM - Return to Cagliari

- As the day draws to a close, make your way back to Cagliari with memories of Porto Flavia and Portixeddu etched in your mind. Reflect on the captivating landscapes and the rich cultural heritage you experienced throughout the day.

Expenses:

- Transportation: €40-€60 (car rental or guided tour)
- Entrance Fee: €10-€15 (Porto Flavia)
- Lunch: €20-€25 (depending on your choice of restaurant)
- Optional: €5 (beach chair rental at Portixeddu)

Santa Teresa Gallura

Morning:

- Start your day early and make your way to Santa Teresa Gallura, a charming coastal town located in the northern part of Sardinia. You can either rent a car or take a bus from nearby towns like Olbia or Alghero. The journey takes approximately one to two hours, depending on your starting point.
- Once you arrive in Santa Teresa Gallura, head straight to the main square, Piazza Vittorio Emanuele, where you'll find several cafés and restaurants. Grab a delicious Italian breakfast consisting of a cappuccino and a freshly baked pastry to kick-start your day.

- After breakfast, take a leisurely stroll along the town's promenade, enjoying the breathtaking views of the Mediterranean Sea. Don't forget to visit the iconic Torre di Longosardo, a historic tower that offers panoramic views of the coastline.

Afternoon:

- For lunch, explore the local cuisine by indulging in some fresh seafood dishes. Santa Teresa Gallura is renowned for its seafood, so make sure to try specialties like spaghetti alle vongole (clam spaghetti) or grilled fish.
- After lunch, head to Rena Bianca Beach, located just a short walk from the town center. This stunning beach boasts crystal-clear turquoise waters and soft white sand, making it the perfect spot to relax and soak up the sun. Take a refreshing

swim in the sea or simply unwind under the shade of an umbrella.

Evening:

- As the day comes to an end, explore the narrow streets of Santa Teresa Gallura's historic center. Admire the colorful buildings adorned with flowers and browse through the local boutiques, offering handmade crafts and souvenirs.
- For dinner, savor traditional Sardinian dishes at one of the town's authentic restaurants. Try the famous Sardinian lamb or porceddu (roasted suckling pig) for a truly authentic culinary experience.

Expenses:

- Transportation: The cost of transportation will depend on your starting point. If you choose to rent a car, prices can range from 40-70 EUR per day. Alternatively, bus tickets from nearby towns may cost around 10-20 EUR round trip.
- Breakfast: Expect to spend around 5-10 EUR for a typical Italian breakfast.
- Lunch: Prices for a seafood lunch can vary depending on the restaurant and dish

chosen. Budget around 15-30 EUR per person.

- Beach: Access to Rena Bianca Beach is free of charge.
- Dinner: Dinner at a local restaurant may cost around 20-40 EUR per person, depending on the menu and drinks.
- Souvenirs: The cost of souvenirs will vary based on your preferences.

PRACTICAL INFORMATION AND TIPS

Transportation in Sardinia

Car Rental

- If you want the freedom to explore Sardinia at your own pace, then renting a car is the best option. There are several car rental companies operating on the island, and you can find cars to suit all budgets. Rental prices start from around €30 per day, but can be higher in peak season.

Public Transportation

- Sardinia also has a good public transportation system, which is operated by ARST. There are buses and trains that connect all the major towns and cities on the island. Public transportation is a more affordable option than renting a car, but it can be less convenient, as the schedules are not always as frequent.

Taxis

- Taxis are available in all the major towns and cities on Sardinia. They are a convenient way to get around, but they can be expensive. Taxi fares start from around €5 for a short journey, and can be much higher for longer trips.

Ferries

- Sardinia is also connected to several other islands by ferry. This is a great way to explore the smaller islands off the coast of Sardinia, such as La Maddalena and Caprera. Ferry fares start from around €10 for a one-way ticket.

Expenses

- Car rental: €30-€100 per day
- Public transportation: €5-€20 per day
- Taxis: €5-€50 per trip
- Ferries: €10-€50 per one-way ticket

Safety and Emergency Contacts

- Be aware of your surroundings, especially in crowded areas or at night.
- Keep your valuables close to you and do not leave them unattended.
- Be careful when crossing the street, as drivers may not be as aware of pedestrians as they are in other countries.
- If you are hiking or camping, be sure to let someone know where you are going and when you expect to be back.
- Drink bottled water and avoid swimming in areas where there are signs warning of dangerous currents.

Here are some emergency contacts in Sardinia:

- Police: 112
- Ambulance: 118
- Fire department: 115

- Tourist information: 110

The cost of medical care in Sardinia can be expensive, so it is a good idea to have travel insurance. You should also be aware of the cost of calling emergency services from your mobile phone.

Currency and Money Matters

The currency in Sardinia is the euro. You can exchange your currency for euros at banks, currency exchange bureaus, and some hotels. You can also use credit and debit cards in most places.

Here are some tips for saving money on your trip to Sardinia:

- Stay in a hostel or bed and breakfast.
- Cook your own meals.
- Take advantage of free activities, such as hiking, swimming, and sunbathing.
- Visit off-season.

WiFi and Internet Access

Sardinia is a beautiful island with a lot to offer tourists, from stunning beaches to ancient ruins. And if you're planning a trip, you'll be glad to know that internet access is widely available.

Most hotels, restaurants, and cafes offer free WiFi, and you can also find hotspots in many public places, such as parks, squares, and beaches. The speed of the internet varies, but it's usually fast enough for basic tasks like checking email, browsing the web, and using social media.

If you need to use the internet for more demanding tasks, such as streaming videos or downloading large files, you may want to consider getting a local SIM card. There are several providers to choose from, and prices start at around €10 per month.

Here is a breakdown of the average costs of WiFi and internet access in Sardinia for tourists:

- Free WiFi: Most hotels, restaurants, and cafes offer free WiFi.
- Local SIM card: SIM cards start at around €10 per month.

- Data roaming: If you're from outside the EU, you'll likely be charged for data roaming.
- Tips for staying connected in Sardinia:
- Check your hotel's WiFi policy: Some hotels have a limit on the amount of data you can use, so be sure to check the policy before you start using the internet.
- Use public hotspots wisely: Public hotspots can be slow, so avoid using them for demanding tasks.
- Get a local SIM card: If you need to use the internet for more demanding tasks, getting a local SIM card is a good option.
- Be aware of data roaming charges: If you're from outside the EU, you'll likely be charged for data roaming.

Travel Insurance

There are a few reasons why travel insurance is so important in Sardinia. First, the cost of medical care in Sardinia can be very high. If you were to get sick or injured while you were there, you could easily rack up a bill of thousands of euros. Travel insurance would cover the cost of your medical care, so you wouldn't have to worry about paying for it out of pocket.

Second, travel insurance can also cover you for other expenses, such as lost luggage, trip cancellation, and emergency medical transportation. If your luggage were to get lost, travel insurance would reimburse you for the cost of replacing your belongings. And if you had to cancel your trip for a covered reason, travel insurance would reimburse you for your non-refundable travel expenses.

Here are some of the expenses that travel insurance typically covers in Sardinia:

- Medical expenses
- Emergency medical transportation
- Trip cancellation
- Baggage loss or damage
- Canceled or delayed flights
- Personal liability
- Legal expenses

The cost of travel insurance will vary depending on the length of your trip, your age, and your health. However, it's usually a relatively small price to pay for the peace of mind that it provides.

Useful Phrases and Etiquette

Useful Phrases

- Hello: Buongiorno (bohn-jorno)
- Goodbye: Arrivederci (ar-ree-veh-deer-chee)
- Please: Per favore (pair fah-vor-ay)
- Thank you: Grazie (gra-tsyeh)
- You're welcome: Prego (preh-goh)
- Excuse me: Scusi (skoo-zee)
- Do you speak English? Parla inglese? (pahr-lah een-gleh-zeh)
- I don't understand: Non capisco (non kah-pee-skoh)
- Where is the bathroom? Dove è il bagno? (doh-veh eh eel bah-nyoh)
- How much does this cost? Quanto costa? (kwan-toh koh-stah)

Etiquette

- When entering a shop or restaurant, it's customary to say "buongiorno" to the shopkeeper or waiter.
- Tipping is not expected in Sardinia, but it is appreciated. A small tip of a few euros is sufficient.
- When dining out, it's common to share dishes. This is especially true if you're ordering antipasti or pasta.

- Sardinians are very proud of their culture and heritage. It's considered polite to learn a few basic phrases in Italian before you visit.

Expenses for Tourists

- Accommodation: A hostel bed will cost around €20 per night, while a budget hotel will cost around €50 per night.
- Food: A three-course meal at a mid-range restaurant will cost around €30.
- Activities: A day trip to a nearby beach or town will cost around €20.
- Transportation: A bus ticket within a city will cost around €1.

Sardinia Travel Journal

My Travel Journal

Date: ____________ Time: ____________

Adventure Checklist For This Trip

Places:

Notes

Itinerary

Address

Location	Hotel	Activity	Time

Destination	Transportation

Budget plan

	Transportation	Lodging	Food	Others
Budget				
Actual				
Difference				

Accommodation

Name:

Address

Of Nights

Dates Bookeds

Check In

Check Out

Booking

Total Cost

Website

Schedule

1
2
3
4
5
6
7
8
9

Notes

Printed in Great Britain
by Amazon

27411769R00090